W9-BPN-886

# ROBERT'S RULES

## *QuickStart Guide*®

The Simplified Beginner's Guide
to Robert's Rules of Order

**ClydeBank Business**

Editors: Marilyn Burkley
Cover Illustration and Design: Katie Donnachie, Copyright © 2016 by ClydeBank Media LLC
Interior Design & Illustrations: Katie Donnachie, Copyright © 2016 by ClydeBank Media LLC

First Edition - Last Updated: October 4, 2022

For bulk sales inquiries, please visit www.clydebankmedia.com/orders, email us at orders@clydebankmedia.com, or call 888-208-6826. Special discounts are available on quantity purchases by corporations, associations, and others.

Copyright © 2016
www.clydebankmedia.com
All Rights Reserved

ISBN-13: 978-1-945051-02-9

# PRAISE FOR

## QuickStart Guides.

Really well written with lots of practical information. These books have a very concise way of presenting each topic and everything inside is very actionable!

— ALAN F.

My new book is so helpful, it's so easy to understand and I can recommend it to any client no matter what level of expertise they have (or don't have).

— AMANDA K.

Everything is written in a beautiful font which is great for people who get bored with reading.

— ANGEL L.

I appreciated how accessible and how insightful the material was and look forward to sharing the knowledge that I've learned.

— SCOTT B.

My new QuickStart Guide is very easy to follow, it's really well written and it breaks everything down, especially the essentials.

— ARIZE O.

After reading this book, I must say that it has been one of the best decisions of my life!

— ROHIT R.

This book is one-thousand percent worth every single dollar!

— HUGO C.

This is a "go-to" book for not only beginners but also as a refresher for experienced practitioners.

— CHARLES C.

I finally understand this topic ... this book has really opened doors for me!

— MISTY A.

# Contents

# BEFORE YOU START READING, DOWNLOAD YOUR FREE DIGITAL ASSETS!

 **Helpful Motions Cheat Sheet**

 **Sample Minutes Reporting Form**

 **Governing Documents Reference**

 **Sample Meeting Agenda**

## TWO WAYS TO ACCESS YOUR FREE DIGITAL ASSETS

Use the camera app on your mobile phone
to take a picture of the QR code or visit the link below
and instantly access your digital assets.

 SCAN ME

or

www.clydebankmedia.com/roberts-assets

 VISIT URL

# Introduction

There's surely a reason that meetings are often synonymous with wasted time, frustration, annoyance, and dread. Consider this hypothesis: we are disillusioned with meetings because they should, in theory, be useful, vibrant, and enlightening, but too often, in practice, they prove anything but. Humans make the mistake of thinking that language development makes us different from animals. It really bums us out to find that, even with our complex brains and our capacity to verbally crystallize our ideas, we still find ourselves talking past one another, unable to listen and unable to effectively integrate our good ideas together into a whole greater than its parts.

The sad truth is that when too many big brains are in one room, they're likely to suffer wasteful clashes of ego when they should be bursting at the seams with brilliant ideas. Ineffective meetings make us cynical. They ridicule our belief in teamwork and reinforce the unhealthy belief that we can't trust anyone but ourselves when it comes to getting stuff done—truly a toxic outlook in a cooperative work environment. We're disillusioned with meetings because they dangle the prospect of progress in our faces, before quickly exposing the pettiness and frailty of the human ego. Successful organizations and businesses don't thrive on cynicism, they suffer from it. So what's to be done?

US Army Colonel Henry Martyn Robert created the Robert's Rules of Order as a guidebook in the late 19th century. Its original title was Pocket Manual of Rules of Order for Deliberative Assemblies.

**NOTE**

Robert's Rules of Order is now in its 11th incarnation as of 2011, and its formal title is Robert's Rules of Order Newly Revised 11th Edition.

Colonel Robert's purpose was to derive an everyday methodology from formal parliamentary procedure. Since its inception, Robert's Rules of Order has become synonymous with formal parliamentary procedure. Be that as it may, the original pocket manual—though modeled after the rules used in the US House of Representatives—was intended for bodies much less formal. In fact, the impetus for the creation of Robert's Rules of Order was a public meeting held at the most humble of venues, a church.

Upon being asked to preside over this meeting, it occurred to Colonel Robert—then 26 years of age— that he was at a complete loss for procedural know-how. Nonetheless, as legend has it, he tried to wing his way through the meeting much to his own chagrin and embarrassment. After enduring the humiliation of presiding over a civic body without experience, Colonel Robert vowed never again to return to such a post until he'd taken the time to learn about parliamentary procedure.

Robert's autodidactic pursuit, however, would soon grow legs when he realized how badly a unified, written body of meeting procedure was needed. As a military man, the Colonel regularly toured various locales throughout the country and discovered that the guidelines followed during formal meetings varied tremendously from place to place. Vividly seeing the need for a standardized authority on a layman's parliamentary procedure, Colonel Robert penned his now famous work.

**NOTE** The Colonel was no stranger to the pen. As an engineer, he'd authored two other works of technical writing: The Water-Jet as an Aid to Engineering Construction (1881), and Analytical and Topical Index to the Reports of the Chief of Engineers and the Officers of the Corps of Engineers (compiled from 1866-1879 and published in 1881).

Robert's supposition was quickly validated. Ordinary societies needed a standard-bearing rule book to help govern their organizational detail and meetings. Upon publication, the book skyrocketed into public consciousness. Millions of copies were sold and distributed, and they continue to be to this day. Since its initial publication in 1876, Robert's Rules of Order has undergone two revisions and has been issued in a total of 11 editions. The most recent edition of the book, published in 2011, Robert's Rules of Order Newly Revised 11th Edition, includes a revision that accounts for modern phenomena that affect organizational behavior, such as the provisions for incorporating video and tele-conferencing into your formal meetings, as well as the role of email and other present-day practices.

This book focuses on interpreting and simplifying Robert's Rules of Order as they are set forth in the most recent, 2011 revision. In adherence to the original spirit of Robert's Rules, this book is intended to be used by ordinary societies as a practical utility for more productive (and shorter) meetings, to define a strong organizational structure, and to protect valuable minority voices that, without rules of order, are apt to be drowned out by the volume and bluster of the biggest ego in the room.

This book is the ideal companion for civic and professional groups, volunteer organizations, PTAs, home and property owners' associations, motorcycle clubs and more. If you've got a bare bones grasp on parliamentary procure and want to fill in the blanks with useful details, then this book will help. This book will also prove a valuable resource if you've recently been appointed to a position of responsibility in your organization and you're looking to add professionalism, dignity, and efficiency to your group-level operations.

**NOTE** Unlike the 19th century (and finely technical) language of our source text, this book articulates the practical application of Robert's Rules of Order in common language.

# | 1 |
# Setting Up for Success

This chapter discusses how Robert's Rules guide the establishment of a new organization. Before you decide whether you need to read this chapter first or skip ahead, consider the following two factors:

1. If you're participating in or presiding over a brand new organization, then this is a good place to start reading.

2. If you're presiding over an organization with established but problematic or undisciplined procedure and you want to give your organization a fresh start, then this chapter is a good place to begin. Just be careful that you don't lose sight of the things your organization is doing correctly. As the townsfolk say, "Even a broken clock is right twice a day." And, as the townsfolk have also been known to say "Don't throw the baby out with the bath water."

## Calling the 1st Organizational Meeting

You've identified a charitable cause, a political purpose, or some other reason to organize, and now you're ready to exercise your First Amendment right to assemble. Maybe you've had it up to your eyeballs with the way the state has neglected the local wildlife preserves, and you're ready to organize some civic opposition, or maybe you're concerned about a developer who wants to demolish a historically significant landmark and erect a new gaggle of gaudy condominiums. Maybe you already own your own gaudy condominium and are leading the way to establishing an active property owners' association to protect the value of your collectivized dwelling structures. The point is this: your first organizational meeting, and all who attend it, should have a unified objective or purpose in mind.

In Robert's Rules this is known as a ***mass meeting***, which refers to an unorganized group that is bound together only by a shared goal. In this case, the shared goal, in the broadest sense, is to establish an organization. But seeing as officers have yet to be appointed/elected and ***bylaws*** have yet to be established, this introductory meeting is still considered a mass meeting.

Since your introductory meeting lacks most all formalities, you're free to simply invite whom you choose and select a location you feel is appropriate.

## Electing Temporary Officers During The 1st Meeting

The first *order of business* is to nominate temporary officers for the organization. Temporary officers are installed to serve until officers can be the formally elected. During the first meeting for many organizations, the individual who *called* the meeting is generally seen as spearheading the effort. If you're reading this, then that individual is likely *you*.

Here's the deal—if you want to establish a tone for order in this group from the get-go, then you should offer to elect a temporary *chairman*, also known as a *chairman pro tem*, for this first organizational meeting. Though you will likely get the spot (being the coordinator, guide, and tip of the spear), the process will give the rest of your group a sense of the way things will operate moving forward. And, hopefully, they'll be impressed. It's up to the chairman to call for the election of other temporary officers. If it's important—by the chairman's discretion—to record the details of this meeting, then perhaps a *secretary pro tem* is in order. If there's going to be a collection of funds at any point during or after this organizational meeting, then a treasurer pro tem is a good idea, too.

## The Resolution for a Permanent Association

Here's where things truly go from 'we're just talking about something we're all concerned about' to 'we intend to unify our energies and prepare to take action.' For the many people who find meetings frustrating because they usually turn out to be a lot of talk with hardly any action, introducing a resolution for a permanent association will win the confidence of your meeting attendees. It will also show those both inside and outside your up-and-coming organization that you have resolve and intent.

You should have the **Resolution for Permanent Association** written down beforehand. As the chairman pro tem, you're going to allow some discussion on the matter at hand from amongst the attendees of your mass meeting. At this point, in the absence of any formal agreed-upon procedure, use your best judgment to police the meeting. Make sure that no one sucks all the oxygen out of the room, and make sure the meeting stays on track. After everyone with concerns has had the chance to voice them, then you (or a friend you've got waiting in the wings) should introduce the Resolution to Form a Permanent Association.

This resolution is not complicated. It should read to the following effect: "Resolved: Given the concerns expressed in this meeting, an association should be formed to address _____." You can make the resolution more pertinent to the issue at hand, but it need not be too fancy.

Once the resolution is introduced to the group, the chairman handles it as he would any other *motion* (the handling of motions is covered in depth in Chapter 4).

## Your Organization Needs Bylaws ASAP

Many organizations make the mistake of neglecting to establish bylaws early on. Common sense is good, but, as you probably know, it's not that common. This especially holds true when groups of people get together and try to think and act as one. Without bylaws, the members of your organization are much more likely to carry disparate notions of the group's plans and operating norms. Making sure that everyone is on the same page is one of the key components to a successful concerted effort, and this is one of the earliest and most crucial steps to that effect.

Bylaws will be discussed in more detail in the following chapter. For now, it's important to know that you're going to need them, and that the best way to get your bylaws established is to appoint a committee responsible for drafting them. As the chairman pro tem, you can appoint the individuals whom you wish to serve on the bylaw drafting committee. Select individuals who are good thinkers and writers. You should also favor individuals for this committee who are capable of donating a good amount of their time (in the short term) to the organization—drafting bylaws can be time-intensive. The process requires research, thought, revision, and in some cases even material expense. If there are going to be expenses incurred through the production of this draft, like copying or research expenses, then propose a resolution to reimburse the bylaw drafting committee for any or a set amount of expenses incurred.

When attempting to institute an effective system of order, such as Robert's Rules, there will likely be some members of your organization who see adherence to procedure, such as the formal allocation of smaller expenses, as a waste of time. They may urge you to let what they perceive as 'smaller issues' be governed with less formality. There are numerous ways to handle the complaints of these individuals. You can succinctly state that it's important to get the organization in the habit of responsible and transparent money and resource management. After all, the magnitude of funds and resources the organization commands will likely increase over time, and starting with a scalable system now will save effort down the road. Deal with the less important formalities of your procedure expediently, but never let it dissolve into a free-for-all. Order may not always appear perfectly efficient, but in the long run, it's always more fruitful than an unbridled and uncontrolled assembly.

Take a little bit of time near the end of the meeting to allow the entire group—not just the newly appointed bylaw committee—to weigh in on what should go into the bylaws. The content and nature of your bylaws will differ from group to group, depending on factors such as group size and financial position (see the next chapter for more details). Remember, you've now got a committee devoted exclusively to creating your organization's bylaws. Don't beat the subject to death in this first meeting. Give the committee time to do its job.

## Wrapping Up

Don't forget to set a time and place for the next meeting in which the bylaws committee will present its draft to the group. Your bylaws committee members should contribute, obviously, when deciding on an appropriate date. Their job is front-and-center at the moment, and what they produce will have far-reaching consequences for your newly-formed organization.

# | 2 |
# Building Your Bylaws

Whether you're beginning a brand new organization or looking to establish better law and order in your existing one, this chapter will guide you through the process of using Robert's Rules to create smart bylaws.

## The Power is Yours!

An organization is an organization is an organization, whether it's a government responsible for millions of citizens, a trade guild looking out for the interests of a specific industry, or a group of mothers who are concerned about adolescent drug use in the community. When it comes to setting bylaws for your organization, there's not really a lot of limitation. Your organization's members can and must agree on whatever bylaws they want to use.

Though bylaws give organizations a great deal of creative power, **parliamentary law** provides some agreed-upon fundamentals of managing **deliberative assemblies**. If you're reading this book, then you probably have a keen interest in what 'parliamentary law' entails. Listed on page 19 you will find the basics of parliamentary law that should hold true in any venue where parliamentary procedure or Robert's Rules are recognized.

## The Importance of Rules

If you're going to act through an 'organization,' or, put another way, allow an 'organization' to act on your behalf, then there must be a reasonable framework that's transparent and intelligible to all the organization's members and that clearly defines how the organization is authorized to act. Using Robert's Rules allows you to set up a Rule of Law within your organization that will ultimately make your organization stronger, as its members *recognize* its actions, even when certain of those members are not in direct support of said actions.

A key point that all practitioners of parliamentary procedure should remember is that the rules exist to serve an assembly in the execution of their duties and their will, not the other way around. While structures like Robert's

Rules can guide your organization toward fair, orderly, and reasonable action, you must never forget that the rules aren't the point of assembly. The point of assembly is your PTA, or you neighborhood association, or your club. The change that your organization wants to affect is the point of the rules, and they exist to expedite the process while ensuring order and a fair representation of your organization's membership.

> *Parliamentary law should be the servant, not the master, of the assembly.*
> – HENRY M. ROBERT

## The Difference Between Bylaws & Rules of Order

What an organization uses as its 'rules of order' are generally set forth and specified in its bylaws. The difference between the two is that bylaws are customized, usually drafted at the local level, to govern the behavior of an organization, while rules of order are primarily concerned with ensuring that meetings are conducted in a just and organized fashion. Rules of order can be customized and tweaked to accommodate the group using them.

For example, if a group decides that motions can only pass with a unanimous vote, as opposed to just a majority vote, then a *special rule of order* can be written into the bylaws or simply declared. A special rule of order denotes a specified exception to the rules of order currently in action (such as Robert's Rules).

Many organizations tend to organically develop certain ways of doing things that aren't noted in the bylaws or in the rules of order. These habits are known as "customs" and, like the written rules, should always be followed until a motion is advanced to challenge them. Again, this is based on the principle that the more consistency you can achieve when running your *deliberative assembly* the better. Consistency creates a uniform expectation and predictability (in a good way) for your organization.

Organizations are often used to establish other organizations. And the founding or parent organization often issues what's known as a *charter*, which is used to govern the operation of the subordinate organization. The rules enshrined in a charter are just as relevant, if not more relevant, than those enshrined in the bylaws. If an organization is operating in accordance with a charter, then only the organization that established the charter is permitted to amend it. The word 'charter' may also be used to refer to an organization's articles of incorporation, as defined by a state authority.

# The Basics of Parliamentary Law

» Groups are run by their members; members have the right to vote, make motions, and otherwise direct the actions of the deliberative assembly.

» Majority rules, but minorities have the right to be heard.

» The only way to prevent someone from being heard (to end a debate) is with a two-thirds majority vote.

» A Larger majority vote is required to change a rule than to establish a rule. This point of parliamentary law is designed to prevent rules from being changed too often on account of how many and which people show up for a meeting.

Sometimes an organization's rules will come into conflict with one another. For example, let's say you start putting down your bylaws and you want to institute a provision that allows for absent members to relay their votes through other, present members. This is known as voting by proxy and is not valid according to Robert's Rules because individuals who vote must hear any new information that is presented during the meeting leading up to the vote. So, if the same organization that writes voting by proxy into its bylaws also relies on Robert's Rules as its rules of order, which authority takes precedence?

Let's say, for example, that our organization is a local PTA; its bylaws have been drafted and approved, and it's been agreed upon that Robert's Rules will inform the PTA's rules of order. The PTA has elected (or hired) a **parliamentarian** to oversee adherence to the rules of order, and the parliamentarian learns that the bylaws are in conflict with Robert's Rules. What happens?

The answer is that the bylaws are upheld and voting by proxy is allowed in the PTA. Bylaws always supersede rules of order. In fact, bylaws supersede all other authorities with the exception of charters. Charters are pretty much immovable. Let's break it down—Figure 1 shows the hierarchy of authority.

**NOTE** Another rule-type that is discussed in Robert's Rules is the standing rule. Standing rules are created when the group recognizes a need for a rule not explicitly specified in the prevailing bylaws, charter, or rules of order. A standing rule is voted in by a majority and remains in effect until the group suspends or abolishes it. In the hierarchy in figure 1, standing rules would be placed below bylaws but above rules of order, right on par with special rules of order. A standing rule can be suspended, modified, or abolished only at a point during a meeting when the rule is wielded. So, if there's a standing rule to disallow chewing gum in your bike club meeting, then the abolishment, suspension, or change to that rule may only be brought up if a member of the group is chewing gum or about to chew gum.

## 1 CHARTERS

- Not even the bylaws can supersede the rules established by a charter.
- This is by necessity; if bylaws could outrank charter provisions, then any subsidiary organization could operate completely autonomous from its parent organization. It would be anarchy.

## 2 BYLAWS

- The advantage of having bylaws high on the food chain is that the group will generally be more familiar with its bylaws than with its rules of order.
- This is because, in most cases, the group itself authors the bylaws, whereas the rules of order are generally taken from a third party source, like Robert's Rules.

fig. 1

## 3 SPECIAL RULES OF ORDER

- If special rules of order didn't outrank general rules of order, then there would be no point in creating them.

## 4 RULES OF ORDER

- These could be Robert's Rules or whichever parliamentary authority that is in use.
- Ironically, Robert's Rules places last, ironic because they are actually defining the hierarchy of authority.

The hierarchy of authority.

*Source: Robert's Rules of Order Newly Revised (11th ed.)*

Now that you have an understanding of how the different classes of rules fit together, you can roll up our sleeves and draft some practice bylaws for your organization. A good place to start is with your peers. Identify other groups similar to your own and try and find their bylaws online or contact the other groups' secretary or president to get a copy.

## Bylaws are Serious Business

Bylaws take precedence over all other rules save those in a charter. As noted previously, bylaws are easier to establish than to change. While a simple majority vote adopts and approves your organization's bylaws, any subsequent revisions will require a two-thirds majority.

Bylaws may never be suspended, even if there is a unanimous vote to do so. The only exception to this rule occurs when the bylaw would otherwise qualify as a rule of order, such as when it relates to the procedural behavior of the organization. For example, if the secretary of your organization—who, as required by the bylaws, must document the minutes of your meetings—is absent from a meeting, the bylaw establishing his role may be suspended to allow for someone else to temporarily record the meeting minutes. These exceptions should be assessed scrupulously. If there is any ambiguity about whether a bylaw can be suspended, then the safest play is to disallow the suspension.

## What Bylaws Can & Must Cover

If you're going to use Robert's Rules as your rules of order for parliamentary procedure, then there are going to be certain things that, in most every organization, must be specified in your bylaws. For example, if you're holding elections for vice president and two individuals get the same amount of votes, you'll need to expressly state in your bylaws how to deal with such a situation. Robert's Rules, as they stand, don't have any specific provisions on run-off elections. Figure 2 shows the other common areas in which bylaws are necessary.

---

### VOTING BY PROXY

Without specific expression in the bylaws, members may never vote by proxy, or by telephone or email. This reflects the fact that in order to make an informed decision, voters must have all of the available facts, and the same facts presented to the rest of the attending organization. When absent, their opinions can't be held in the same regard as those in attendance.

---

## VIRTUAL MEETINGS

If you're using Robert's Rules and want to allow meetings to take place via teleconference or video conference, then this provision must be specified in your bylaws.

## SUSPENDING YOUR BYLAWS

The reason that Robert's Rules do not permit bylaws to be suspended, even by unanimous vote, is because this protects the rights of the absentees. In other words, if a member must miss a meeting, she should have the assurance that the meeting will be conducted according to the bylaws in place.

GRAPHIC

fig. 2

## TEMPORARILY CHANGE ELECTION PROCEDURE

In Robert's Rules, you will likely run up against a scenario in which a vote by ballot is technically required, but, in reality, not necessary. Use your bylaws to specify when a vote by ballot is and is not required.

## NON-MEMBER INFLUENCE

Robert's Rules are pretty adamant about an organization's power beginning and ending with its members. If you wish for your organization to be occasionally influenced by non-members, giving non-members voting rights in certain scenarios or even allowing non-memebers to be elected as officers, then these provisions must be specified in your bylaws.

## EXECUTIVE BOARDS

You need to rely on your bylaws when setting the rules and procedures that govern the election and duties of any executive boards in your organization.

# Robert's Rules Bylaw Recipe

Robert's Rules prescribe a specific ordering of key 'articles' that should appear in your bylaws:

a. **Name:** Your organization's official name is specified in this article.

b. **Object:** A couple sentences on the purpose of your organization.

c. **Membership:** This is the first article that's going to require a whole lot of thinking. It needs to cover everything from how membership is established in your organization to how it's lost (through failure to pay dues, breeches in conduct, etc.). If membership in your organization is going to be stratified across multiple different levels, then those levels should be described in this article. In this article you must specify any qualifications that govern whether someone can be a member. For example, if your organization is a PTA, then perhaps this article should specify that a member must either be a parent of a student or a teacher.

The membership article should specify any initiation procedures that must be followed prior to admission into the organization. This article must also specify any financial requirements for the organization, as well as the consequences for delinquency. The article also should specify the extent to which delinquent members lose their rights and how they may be reinstated to the organization (if at all). If the organization is subordinate or superior to another per a charter or constitution, then this article should specify any provisions governing individuals who are members in multiple organizations throughout the hierarchy.

d. **Officers:** What types of officers will you have in your organization? How will they be nominated? What are their duties? How long are their terms? How many times can each officer be reelected to the same position? These are the questions you must answer in this article of your bylaws. If you want to get really specific, then you may have separate articles for each officer position in your organization.

e. **Meetings:** In this article you will need to specify how, when, and by whom your meetings will be scheduled, how notice will be given, and you should also specify if and how special meetings will be convened, through what authority. *Quorums* for your meetings must also be specified in this article.

f. **Executive Board:** This article is extremely important. Executive boards conduct business on behalf of the organization in the time between meetings. They are responsible for the organization's good name, and the methods of their appointments or elections should be carefully considered.

This article must define not only how the executive board is defined, but also the extent of its capacities and powers. Organizations often come across hard times when there are divergent, asymmetrical understandings within the membership about the scope of the executive board's power and privilege. Make sure these elements are well defined within this article. This article should incorporate its own versions of articles D and E, detailing how the officers come to power, how their meetings are scheduled, how quorum is established, etc.

g.  **Committees:** A certain type of committee called a ***standing committee*** can be brought into existence through your organization's bylaws. For example, if your organization is a college fraternity, then you will continually need to acquire new members as graduates depart and the freshman class at your university matriculates in. Therefore, college fraternities might set up a standing 'membership committee' to oversee the recruitment of prospective members.

Each standing committee defined in this article should be imbued with its own version of articles A, B, and C. Each committee should have a name, a few sentences about its purpose, and details of how the committee's membership is to be appointed or elected. If the committee is to wield any specific power, then this too should be specified in the article. If you want to give your organization the ability to expediently create new standing committees, not specified by the original bylaws, then this is the article under which such powers should be defined. If you do not define such powers here, then you will not be able to form another standing committee without amending the bylaws, requiring previous notice and a two-thirds vote.

h.  **Parliamentary Authority:** If you're using Robert's Rules of order, then adding this article to your bylaws shouldn't be much of a problem at all. Just write: "Refer to Robert's Rules of Order Newly Revised 11th Edition as the written authority governing this organization's rules of order."

i.  **Amendment:** Robert's Rules specify that bylaws can be amended only with a two-thirds vote and only after the group is given prior notice that a bylaw change is scheduled for a vote. If you want to change how your bylaws are amended, then you must specify this in this article of your bylaws.

**NOTE** When motions are amended, they usually—according to Robert's Rules—require only a majority vote if notice has been given. If notice has not been given, then the change will require a two-thirds majority. Another way to amend a motion is to acquire a majority of the organization's entire membership. Bylaws are comparatively more difficult to amend.

## Bylaws Should Not Be Easy to Change

Robert's Rules set forth stringent thresholds for changing bylaws to both protect the interests of minority members and to prevent a small group of people from materially changing the structure, direction, or finances of the organization. If a simple voting majority could amend bylaws without notice, then an ill-intentioned cabal could substantially change the entire organization on a random night when the weekly meeting is sparsely attended. Such a coup could change the name of the group, fire the executives, or give themselves control of the group's bank accounts; the worst part is that they could do all this legally, in accordance with the organization's poorly construed bylaws. Be very careful when writing in provisions to your bylaws that make them easier to change.

While at face value it may seem restrictive and inflexible to institute such rigid precautions, ultimately it is in the best interest of the organization's security and longevity. The whole purpose of this exercise is to create a purpose-built and ordered environment that forms the foundation of your organization's operations. Constantly changing the way things are done is counterproductive and exposes the entire organizational structure to risk.

## Bringing in a Pro Parliamentarian

At this point, you've got a newly formed organization, you've had your first meeting, and you've established a committee to present a draft of your bylaws. The bylaw drafting committee meets to discuss the content of the bylaws. After everyone has expressed his or her view, a small sub-committee is appointed (one or two members) who will be charged with writing the first draft of the bylaws.

> *The parliamentarians operate rather like football coaches. They are not allowed on the playing field, and their signals to the players must be well concealed. Their whispered counsels are never printed in the Congressional Record's account of debates.*
>
> −JOSEPH F. O'BRIEN

**NOTE**

At this stage in the process, it can be very helpful to seek out the services of a professional parliamentarian to work with your bylaw drafting committee and subcommittee. Since professional parliamentarians have a sound understanding of parliamentary procedure, and, presumably significant experience participating in parliamentary-style meeting environments, he or she is likely to be aware of what provisions (or lack thereof) can spell trouble for your organization.

When the draft is complete the full bylaw drafting committee should review it before bringing it to the entire membership for formal ratification.

# | 3 |
# Making the Most of Your Meetings

Your organization hasn't even been formally created yet –nor have any members been formally confirmed—and you've already spurred a multitude of meetings. And this is just the beginning. Soon your bylaws will be formally adopted and you'll, presumably, be having meetings on a regular basis. This chapter delves deeply into the phenomenon of productive and engaging meetings. Why we have them, how to survive them, and how adherence to Robert's Rules can help keep them short, sweet, and to the point!

## The Basics of a Meeting

Most meetings have a few things in common. First, you need people to show up, and other than the unlikely method of telepathy, the best way to get attendance at your meetings is to issue timely notices of where and when your meetings will be held. Compared to the time when the first Robert's Rules were written, this is significantly easier with email, messaging, and social media at your disposal.

If you're hosting regular meetings according to your bylaws, then your membership should get into the habit of showing up at a specified date and time. In order for the deliberative outcome of a meeting to accurately portray the will of the group, a certain threshold of membership must be in attendance in order for the group to take certain important actions. This threshold is known as a quorum.

Robert's Rules uses the term "previous notice" when describing notice requirements. You should spell out the rules on the issuance of notice very clearly in your bylaws. Even if you're going to schedule a regular meeting at the same date/time every week/month, it is wise to have your organization's secretary send out an email giving notice of the meeting 24 hours before the meeting commences (plan ahead and get everyone's contact information).

If such a task seems unwarranted for a regularly scheduled, recurring meeting, then consider having the secretary also issue a copy of the minutes from the previous meeting with the email—this way you're providing both notice of the upcoming meeting and helping your members reconnect with the pertinent subject matter.

When deciding on how and when to give notice about your meetings, be sure to consider the frequency of your meetings. If you're only going to have meetings once every three months, then adequate notice (and possibly even RSVPs) will be a lot more important than if you're planning to have weekly meetings. Also consider where your members reside. If people are driving long distances or flying in, then, obviously, an earlier notice (more 'lead time') is more appropriate. Consider the technological savviness of your average member. If your membership is largely made up of senior citizens, then perhaps text messages shouldn't qualify as adequate notice. Specify these things in your bylaws.

**NOTE** According to the most recent edition of Robert's Rules—Robert's Rules of Order Newly Revised 11th Edition—meeting notice via email may be given, but the member must first explicitly consent to receiving email notification.

In addition to providing the minutes from the previous meeting, consider a bylaw stipulating that notice must be served alongside a breakdown of the business that's scheduled to be addressed. Depending on the nature of the business, notice may or may not be necessary. For example, if your organization is considering an increase in the required membership dues, then notice is probably a good idea, as your members may want to spend some time looking over their own personal budgets before deciding on whether to support or oppose the measure. If the meeting is going to be about less consequential matters, then perhaps no specification need be given in the notice. Distinctions between business items that warrant and do not warrant notice should be defined in the organization's bylaws.

**NOTE** In Robert's Rules, the term call or 'call of the meeting' is used as a more formal way to refer to notice. According to Robert's Rules, the notice should be given in writing, and if the meeting is a special meeting (see section below), then the items to be discussed must be made clear in the notice.

# Regular Meetings

The fundamental building block of most organizations is the *regular meeting*. A regular meeting occurs on an ongoing basis, yearly, monthly, or weekly. The frequency and dates for the regular meeting are usually set in the bylaws—though they can be established in the group's *standing rules*. Standing rules usually set the times and locations of the meetings, as they're more likely to change over time. Regular meetings are open to all members—as opposed to just **board** members or special committee members—and as an assembly, the group discusses and votes on issues relevant to the group. Figure 3 shows common authority on aspects of regular meetings. The charter (highest authority, more difficult to change) sets the frequency of regular meetings, while the standing rules (easier to change, lower authority) set aspects that are more likely to change.

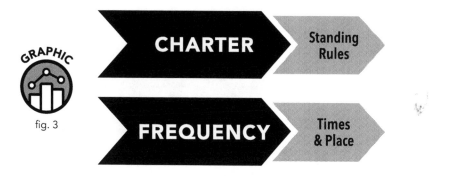

fig. 3

## Special Meetings

Special meetings, also known as 'called meetings,' are set up when the regular meeting schedule is unable to accommodate a specific concern that must be addressed. For example, if a condominium owner's association is facing a costly repair to their shared dwelling structure, and a contractor contacts the group's chairman requesting an immediate yes or no decision on a proposed work quote, then the chairman may call a special meeting so the members can vote on whether to accept or make a counter offer to the contractor's proposal.

> *If the Chair is an effective leader—focusing on the members, treating each fairly, earning everyone's trust—then the meeting will be successful.*
> — HUGH CANNON

**NOTE**

Sure, the group chairman or president should be able to call a special meeting, but what if the chairman just suddenly abandons his post, or gets arrested, or is in serious disagreement with others in the group about the need for a special meeting? What if the chairman betrays or steals from the group? As a best practice, your bylaws should give a few different officers the authority to call a special meeting.

When giving notice that a special meeting is going to happen, the notice must always be given within a reasonable time frame and must include the time and place of the meeting and the specific matter at hand. Not only should this be outlined in your bylaws as a matter of course, but it is simply a prudent measure to ensure that your members come to the meeting armed with knowledge. At the bare minimum, it means that everyone at the meeting is on the same page.

The requirement that an officer calling a special meeting gives clear notice to the matters scheduled for deliberation is a serious mandate. Even if the notice leaves an open clause at the end, such as: "The purpose of the meeting is to discuss a recent offer for roof repair services submitted by xyz Contractors along with various other matters affecting the organization," those "various other matters" are not recognized as valid according to Robert's Rules. Keeping the topics of special meetings stringently focused prevents abuses. An officer might call a meeting in which "various other matters" may be discussed, and members may choose not to attend because the stated topic isn't relevant to them. Meanwhile, the "various other matters" may be extremely relevant to them. For this reason, the intentions of all special meetings must be clearly specified. Any motions or rulings made on non-disclosed topics during a special meeting may subsequently be deemed null and void.

## Adjourned Meetings

To understand *adjourned meetings* you have to understand the basic concept of a session. A *session* refers to a series of meetings that have been designed to focus on a specific order of business. For example, a legislative session, is made up of a multitude of meetings intended to *debate* and pass new laws and so forth. Adjourned meetings happen when a regular or special meeting is formally concluded before a particular order of business has been resolved. For example, if the agreed upon time for a PTA meeting is 7pm to 9pm, and at 9pm a motion is still being vigorously discussed and has yet to come to a vote, then the group may schedule an adjournment meeting to finish the order of business that's incomplete. When an adjourned meeting is called to order, the minutes from the previous meeting are read, then the meeting picks up exactly where the previous meeting left off.

Returning to the example of a PTA meeting, the debate being held was whether or not the time of the organization's regular meetings should be moved to 6pm to 8pm, as opposed to 7pm to 9pm. An adjourned meeting allows for a pertinent order of business to be addressed before the next regular meeting.

**NOTE** When whole sessions are scheduled in advance, you may also use the term 'adjourned meeting' to describe each successive meeting after the first. Technically speaking, every meeting within a formal session, other than the first, constitutes an adjournment of the previous meeting.

# Annual Meetings

Depending on the type of organization, *annual meetings* may take on a very distinct character. Consider, for example, a public company, Corporate Inc. According to the corporation's bylaws (articles of incorporation), it is to host a meeting every year in the form of a deliberative assembly, open to the members of the group (stockholders). During this one annual meeting, the executive board members give their reports about the health and goals of the company and field questions and discussions. After the annual meeting concludes, the executive board members go back to their posts and continue with the work of running the company. This type of organization does not use regular meetings.

Now consider a civic organization, such as the Rotary Club. Even though they have bi-weekly or monthly regular meetings, they still may have an annual meeting. Perhaps at this meeting the officers of the club give their annual, big-picture reports, and the membership nominates and elects new officers along with performing whatever other club duties that demand attention only once a year. Perhaps it's written into the bylaws that the club must take a vote each year as to whether they're satisfied with their meeting venue, their clubhouse, their company logo, the amount they pay in dues, and other issues that don't need to be brought to the table every meeting, but are worth taking a look at on an annual basis.

# Executive Sessions

*Executive sessions* are quite easy to understand. Holding an executive session basically means "members only." Most board meetings and committee meetings are held via an executive session, though the board or committee is free to invite outside attendees as long as bylaws permit.

# More on Quorums

If you defer to Robert's Rules, then a quorum is achieved when a majority of the organization's members show up to attend a meeting. A quorum is the minimum number of meeting attendees you must have to conduct business on behalf of the organization. You can always tinker with quorum requirements in your bylaws—just make sure that the integrity of the organizational structure isn't compromised and that your changes don't challenge the minority voice.

It is, however, a good idea to insert some provisions on chronically absent group members so they don't continuously imperil your group's chances at reaching quorum. Perhaps, if a member misses so many meetings, his or her membership and voting rights are temporarily suspended. There are a lot of ways to tinker with your quorum requirements in your bylaws. You can choose whether to set your quorum based on a percentage turnout of active members or based on a raw number of members. A lot of groups find that the best method for establishing a quorum that makes sense for their group is not readily apparent to them until the group's been conducting business for some time, long enough to develop a meaningful track record.

There's nothing wrong with using the 'wait and see' approach when it comes to setting your quorum. Since it's generally easier to add new bylaws than to change existing ones, a best practice is to use the quorum levels that your rules of order specify (if you're using Robert's Rules, then that would be a majority of your group's members), and then add optimal quorum provisions to your bylaws when the time is right.

## Failing to Make Quorum, What Options Do You Have?

First of all, if you're going with the majority of membership threshold as specified in Robert's Rules and are beginning to fail to make your quorums, then it's important that you take action to adjust the situation sooner rather than later. Otherwise, if you continue to admit new members, the quorum threshold will continue to rise, and it will be that much more difficult to get a quorum together so that you can do something about your quorum problems.

The solution, of course, is an amendment to the bylaws that sets a quorum threshold that makes sense for your organization. If you find yourself in a meeting in which the quorum has not been attained, it's not the end of the world. In fact, there are a few things that you can do. Figure 4 shows some options you still have.

These motions can be heard and debated without a quorum being present. More details on how motions are processed are in the following chapter. The important thing to remember is to take action as soon and as effectively as possible. Don't let too many meetings go by in which you and the other group members are stuck not meeting quorum. Morale will sink and the group will risk being dissolved, which is ironic considering that passing a motion to dissolve requires a quorum. Ironic or not, at this point it should be fairly obvious why a quorum would be needed for dissolution.

GRAPHIC

fig. 4

## MOTION TO ADJOURN

You can call it a day and try again next time. This approach will work when you occasionally can't reach your quorum requirements, but it won't solve chronic issues of absenteeism.

## FIX THE TIME AT WHICH TO ADJOURN

This allows you to set up an adjournment meeting and buys you some time to get the members you need to satisfy your quorum requirement. This time could be before the next regular meeting if the business should be addressed sooner rather than later.

## MOTION TO RECESS

Sometimes your meeting may start with a quorum, but when it comes time to vote on an important issue, you suddenly don't have a quorum anymore. A motion to recess can be used to go track down the missing members and drag them back to the meeting so you can vote.

## FORM A QUORUM CHASING COMMITTEE

You can raise a motion to form a committee responsible for departing the meeting and tracking down enough missing members to attain quorum. This can be done via telephone calls, door-to-door, kidnapping and extortion, etc. While your organization's bylaws (or your state laws for that matter) may not allow kidnapping and extortion, it can sometimes seem as though those methods are the only way to get a reliable turnout.

If there's an emergency and an action must be taken right away that would ordinarily require the presence of a quorum, then you and the other members of the group may take the action, but, for all legal intent and purpose, you are taking the action personally. You are not acting on behalf of the group, and as such, you are taking action at your own risk.

If you're making a purchase for the group, then be warned. In order to be reimbursed, your emergency actions need to be ratified at the next meeting at which a quorum of members is present. Ratification is a term used in Robert's Rules to refer to the group's after-the-fact approval of an action taken without proper authority. If they refuse to *ratify* your expense, then you will be left footing the bill.

# Setting an Agenda

Robert's Rules provides a template for how your meeting's order of business or agenda can be structured. The template may be a little overdone for some organizations, while others may find that they need to add even more elements. Here's the rundown:

## Step 1: A Call to Order

The meeting begins with the presiding officer issuing a single rap of the gavel, letting everyone know that everything that follows, until adjournment, is official group business.

## Step 2: Opening Ceremonies

If you've ever seen characterized representations of what happens behind closed doors at the Elk's Lodge, with the donning of ridiculous hats and unified choruses of nonsense, then what you've seen, technically, constitutes the second step of a meeting being run in accordance with Robert's Rules. This is the step in which any opening songs, hymns, chants, and other ritualistic matters commence. If your organization says the pledge of allegiance or the Hail Mary, step two is where you do it.

## Step 3: Roll Call

The third item on the agenda, as per Robert's Rules, is the roll call. Either the presiding officer or the secretary—whomever your organization appoints—calls the names of expected attendees, and they answer back (hopefully). Not all organizations require a roll call. Robert's Rules suggest that if you're going to practice a roll call, then this part of the meeting is a good place to get it done.

## Step 4: Consent Calendar

The fourth item is a powerful, but somewhat rare, meeting artifact. A consent calendar is a listing of several small items that, though they technically require formal approval by the group, are too small and trivial to warrant placement within the normal order of business.

Therefore, the items are all compiled on the consent calendar before the meeting begins, and the members are able to adopt the items in one, efficient, fell stroke. The consent calendar is usually not used with smaller, less formal organizations, but you'll find it employed in the halls of Congress.

## Step 5: Standard Order of Business

This is the meat of the meeting, in which everything important is decided. A lot is included in this step of the meeting process:

1. The minutes from the previous meeting must be approved. This is usually accomplished by reading them, or at least summarizing them, then making a motion to approve them.

2. Reports are heard from the group's standing committees, boards, and officers. These groups and individuals are usually doing work on the group's behalf outside of the regular meeting, therefore it's a good idea for the general membership to hear their updates before voting begins on old and new business. If the members weren't updated until after the vote, how could they be sure that they made an informed decision?

3. Reports are heard from the group's special committees. Just as with the committees mentioned in the previous step, special committees have presumably been working on behalf of the specific initiatives that warranted their initial formation. These committees are heard from after the groups mentioned in the previous step.

4. Special orders are heard next. *Special orders* refer to items of business that—by way of the bylaws or by a motion—are scheduled to be handled at a certain meeting.

Consider the collegiate Greek college systems of University X. University X is going to hold the annual Greek inter-athletic competition during the last week of May. As such, Fraternity Y decides to institute a special order mandating that competitors for the competition will be nominated and selected during the first meeting in May.

5.  Next, all *general orders* of business are attended to. General orders of business refer to items that were either being discussed when the previous meeting was adjourned or were deliberately postponed for discussion at a later time.

6.  Finally, the floor is open to bring up new business. This mainly means that new motions are ready to be heard.

# | 4 |
# The Art of the Motion

*Motions* are debated, voted on, amended, and otherwise thrown around in most parliamentary systems, including Robert's Rules. They are, in fact, the lifeblood of parliamentary process, the vehicle through which everything else flows. Robert's Rules are riddled with various types of motions that can be advanced and tinkered with in a whole host of scenarios. This chapter focuses on the basics, enough to get your organization up and running strong.

## A Motion is a Motion is a Motion: Not Exactly

Motions made during a deliberative assembly (meeting) come in a few different types, beginning with the *main motion* (figure 5), which is essentially a call to action on a certain business item.

### A MOTION TO MAKE A FINANCIAL ALLOCATION

The organization should purchase an asset, hire a contractor, invest in a stock, donate to a charity, put aside money for a committee within the organization, or otherwise spend funds.

### A MOTION TO ISSUE AN OPTION OF JUDGEMENT

The motion to issue an option of judgement on behalf of group can censure the organization's vice president for making a racially insensitive comment, or enable the organization to formally endorse a particular candidate running for public office, for example.

fig. 5

### A MOTION TO CREATE A RULE

Adds a new bylaw to the organization, or creates a rule that's within the organization's sphere of authority, such as a PTA group voting to extend the hours of operation for the school library.

### MOTION TO ADOPT REPORTED RECOMMENDATIONS

Adopts a recommendation, such as one made by an education research committee to not support common core curriculum on grounds specified by the report.

Examples of main motions.

## MOTION TO AMEND

Whereby someone moves to alter the main motion on the table. This can be for any number of reasons, though it should be noted that motions to amend are frequently themselves unable to be the subject of motions to amend as the resulting situation can become quite complex. Motions to amend are often used to add or insert words in a paragraph, strike words from a paragraph, or completely substitute one section or proposal for another. Motions to amend should require a second and should only be debatable if the motion that the motion to amend sees to alter is debatable.

## MOTION TO POSTPONE INDEFINITELY

The motion usually arises when the main motion is controversial or threatens to compromise the unity of the group. Technically, a motion to postpone indefinitely means that group agrees to not decide on the pending main motion at the current time.

## MOTION TO POSTPONE TO A CERTAIN (DEFINITELY)

GRAPHIC

fig. 6

Unlike a motion to postpone indefinitely, this subsidiary motion isn't intended to leave the main motion for dead. It's usually born of practical necessity, such as not having enough time in the scheduled meeting to process the main motion. When a motion to postpone to a certain time is made and passed, the issue is guaranteed to come up again at the time specified.

## MOTION TO LIMIT OR EXTEND THE DEBATE

Main motions are often debated—in accordance with the organization's rules of order—before going to a vote. According to Robert's Rules, each member may take the floor to debate a motion twice. The motion to limit or extend the limit of the debate is, exactly as it sounds, a way to force a vote after a certain amount of time has passed, or a way to allow the debate to proceed beyond the usual dictates set forth by the rules of order.

## MOTION TO LAY ON THE TABLE

This motion is one of the more commonly misunderstood motions described in Robert's Rules. Most people think of "tabling a bill" as a parliamentary tactic to end discussion on a bill. While this may be true in government legislatures, in Robert's Rules of Order the motion to lay on the table is used to bring the group's attention immediately to a matter or motion much more pressing than the one currently being discussed. A motion to lay on the table does put aside the current main motion, but, under Robert's Rules, it should not be used to get rid of an unpopular main motion, but instead to draw necessary attention to a specified, more pressing matter.

Examples of subsidiary motions.

In addition to main motions, there are *subsidiary motions* (figure 6), *privileged motions*, and *incidental motions*—collectively termed *secondary motions*, motions that help process whatever main motion is currently pending before the group.

Subsidiary motions are put forth so that the pending main motion may be more optimally executed. For example, if a main motion is on the floor that is financial in nature, then it may be a good idea for that motion to receive special attention from any financially focused committees currently at large within the organization. As such, a motion to refer to a committee may be made. The motion to send to a committee is also occasionally referred to as a *motion to commit*.

fig. 7

### MOTION TO ADJOURN

While this motion is often used as a privileged motion, it also can be a main motion if used to cut a regular meeting short or to dissolve an assembly. (Who doesn't love this motion? It's time to go home!)

### MOTION TO FIX THE TIME AT WHICH TO ADJOURN

This motion is used when there is business on the floor and you don't want to just go home and wait for the next regular meeting to take care of it. A motion to fix the time at which to adjourn means that the meeting will adjourn, but there will be adjournment meetings set up to take care of pending business before the next regular meeting of the group commences. This motion can be very useful if you've got a main motion that's still being debated and it looks like the group will not be able to address it due to the time constraints of the current meeting. Your motion to fix the time at which to adjourn essentially sets up a guaranteed special meeting during which this main motion may be properly handled.

### MOTION TO CALL FOR THE ORDERS OF THE DAY

Robert's Rules outlines this very useful and important motion for groups that have a bad habit of getting off track. If there has been an agreement to stick to a meeting agenda, or if a particular main motion was suspended definitely to a certain time and, at that time, it's still not being discussed, then a member makes this motion to get back on track. If the orders of the day are not being followed, this motion can be made, even if someone is speaking.

### MOTION TO RAISE A QUESTION OF PRIVILEGE

This usually deals with an issue of comfort. If it's too hot, cold, or noisy for the members to focus their attention on the meeting, then someone may make a motion to raise a question of privilege in order to improve the comfort-level of the group, i.e., turn on the air conditioning, close the window, or bring in some sandwiches.

Examples of privileged motions.

The next type of secondary motion is the privileged motion (figure 7) . Privileged motions are used to help align the formal business of the meeting with here-and-now realities that may be affecting the immediate welfare of the group. A motion to recess, for example, is a privileged motion. Though, unlike a subsidiary motion, the motion to recess has nothing to do with the main motion at hand, it may very well be of immediate importance to a person whose bladder is threatening to get the best of him.

In addition to the motion to recess, with which you're likely fairly familiar, figure 7 shows some additional common privileged motions.

**NOTE**

The motion to fix the time at which to adjourn can also be used to resolve quorum-based difficulties. If the main motion being discussed is important to you and, in the current meeting, there are not enough members present to establish quorum, then this motion gives you a chance to pursue quorum in a special session.

Last but not least: the incidental motions. Incidental motions deal with how your organization's meeting is going to be conducted in terms of its adherence to the rules of order and *special rules of order*. In other words, incidental motions are all about procedure—how elections are run, how votes are cast, how the rules are allowed to bend or be enforced and when. Figure 8 contains many examples of incidental motions.

**NOTE**

In some situations, a matter of interpretation of the rules of order leave the presiding officer without a clear idea as to whether the point of order being raised is valid. During such occasions, the presiding officer may state the matter of confusion and hold a verbal "yay" or "nay" vote to determine which interpretation will stand.

In addition to requests for information, other formal incidental 'request' motions may be made to aid other pursuits. These incidental motions include requests to withdraw a motion—whereby the person who first made a motion can ask for it to be withdrawn—and requests to read papers, whereby a member asks for permission to read written material that's pertinent to the main motion under discussion.

## MOTION TO APPEAL

This motion is used when a member thinks the presiding officer has made an erroneous ruling. According to Robert's Rules, if you don't exercise your right to appeal when you believe the presiding officer is in error, then you've implicitly given up your right to criticize the ruling.

## MOTION TO SUSPEND THE RULES

You've got to know the rules before you break them, but you still, on occasion, have to break them. The motion to suspend the rules allows for business to proceed, even when a bylaw or a rule of order stands in the way. To pass, the motion requires a two-thirds majority vote, and this vote is usually held in conjunction with the original action that prompted the motion. For example, if a member wants to suspend the rules so as to allow her dog to sit in on a meeting session in violation of a 'no pets allowed' bylaw, then the motion to suspend the rules and the motion to allow the dog to sit in on the meeting session functions as the same motion.

## OBJECT TO THE CONSIDERATION MOTION

fig. 8

This motion preempts any discussion from transpiring on a newly moved-for-main motion. In order to use the object to the consideration motion, you must proclaim your objection in the style of a trial attorney; as soon as the question is raised, you stand and say: "I object to the consideration of this question." In the case of this motion, 'the question' refers to the main motion that's being brought up by another member. Once your motion is made, the chair asks for all to stand who want to hear the motion to be discussed. Afterwards, if a two-thirds majority (opposing the discussion) is still possible, the chair invites all to stand who support the motion to object to the consideration of the question. All of that being said, a member who interrupts another member's designated speaking time by calling a question is being disorderly.

## DIVISION OF THE QUESTION

This incidental motion is used when the main motion being presented has too many component parts and would perhaps be better serviced piecemeal. For example, if someone makes a motion to allocate $1,000 to purchase a new refrigerator for the group's clubhouse and to make waffles the group's official breakfast food, there may be a case for moving to divide the question and allow each of the two tenets of the previous motion to be heard independently.

## DIVISION OF THE ASSEMBLY

This motion is used after a vote is taken—usually a verbal yay or nay vote—and a member doubts whether the group recognized by the presiding officer as the majority is in fact the true majority. It's been known to happen in meetings that one faction is simply louder than another, and, as a result, the presiding officer mistakes the noisiest faction for the majority. A motion for a division of the assembly forces a verifiable revote, such as a ballot-based or stand-up vote.

## DIVISION MOTIONS

Incidental motions encompass all motions that govern the way in which voting and vote counting transpires. If a member wishes that a certain vote be conducted in a certain way—by ballot, roll call, etc.—then he may make a motion related to the method of voting. If he wishes to require that a vote be taken at a certain venue, then he may make a motion related to the polls.

## CONSIDER SERIATIM (OR BY PARAGRAPH)

This motion is used when a deliberative assembly is faced with adopting the dictates of a committee recommendation, a body of bylaws, or any other comprehensive, multi-part written text. Rather than force the assembly to come up with a wholesale yay or nay, the consider seriatim motion allows the dictates to be broken down by paragraph so that each section can be adopted, rejected, or amended.

## NOMINATION MOTIONS

When it's time to elect new officers or board members, nomination motions are used to define the where, how, and when of the nominating process. Usually, this originates with someone making a motion to open nominations for a certain position and concludes with someone making a motion to close nominations. Motions may also be made to specify how the nominees for a certain position are to be selected. For example, a member may make a motion that the current secretary produce a short-list of three nominees to be considered for succession into the secretary position. Or, a member may make a motion that a committee be established to determine nominees.

## REQUEST TO BE EXCUSED FROM A DUTY

An accompanying motion to be excused from duty may be used in conjunction with a resignation of an officer, board member, or committee member or chairman. There motions often follow after the group passes a new main motion that expands the duties of the position at hand.

## POINT OF ORDER

The point of order motion is used to establish accurate parliamentary procedure. Anyone may call a point of order for consideration by the presiding officer. From that point, the presiding officer checks the bylaws or rules of order if need be, then he or she makes a ruling. If the presiding officer rules against your point of order and you believe him or her to be mistaken, then you may always appeal.

## MOTION FOR A PARLIAMENTARY INQUIRY

This incidental motion is available to help members clarify certain details of the organization's rules of order or special rules of order. A parliamentary inquiry is different from a point of order because what is sought after is information not a formal ruling. What the presiding officer issues is thus merely an opinion.

Examples of incidental motions.

# Motions in Action

Now that you have an understanding of the different categories of motions, here's a look at how motions function inside a deliberative assembly from inception to end. Depending on the nature of the motion, it may or may not require a *seconding*, it may or may not need to be put in writing, and it may or may not be amendable or debatable.

When Robert's Rules of Order is the group's prevailing source for parliamentary procedure, main motions always require a second, as they can be debated and amended. Remember that seconds are irrelevant if the main motion is not subject to debate or amendment. Main motions must have a majority vote to be passed unless the bylaws state otherwise. If the main motion is directed at changing procedural 'rule of order' rules that are already established, then the motion requires a two-thirds vote to pass.

Here's how a main motion is presented to the assembly when no other business is pending. If your assembly is in the middle of hashing out an amendment or incidental motion pertaining to another main motion, then you need to wait until the deliberations surrounding the current main motion conclude.

When the time is right (or when it's considered "in order") the member making the motion stands up and addresses the presiding officer or "chairman". The chair then recognizes the member using impartial tonality: "The chair recognizes the member from Sandy Ford." Afterwards, the member states, very succinctly, his motion: "Madame Chairman, I move that we hire a gardener to remove the weeds from the flower bed." Unless the motion is incredibly simple, the member making the motion should have a written copy ready to submit to the presiding officer or secretary.

Since the hypothetical garden maintenance motion is a main motion, it requires a seconding. This is issued verbally by any other member of the assembly with: "I second!" or simply "Second!" If no one immediately seconds the motion, the chairman/presiding officer asks: "Is there a second?" If the motion is still without a second, then it isn't discussed and the floor is opened for the next item of business. The method of requiring a second encourages the discussion and the course of the meeting to proceed on track. It also encourages members of the organization to find support for their contributions before putting them forward or limiting contributions solely to worthwhile ideas.

Assuming the motion is seconded, the chairman then states the motion aloud—"We've got a motion on the floor to hire a gardener to get the weeds out of the flowerbed." Next, the chairman opens up the floor for debate: "Is there any debate?"

**NOTE**

It's interesting to note that, up to this point in the life of the motion, its author owns it and can, as such, withdraw or change it without consent from the group. Once the chairman calls for debate on the motion, it is formally in possession of the group. The motion's original author cannot make any amendments to it or withdraw it without a vote. Part of the chairperson's role is to advise the author on ways in which the motion he's brought forth should be changed. The chairperson should do this before he calls for debate, as the motion is a lot more difficult to change after that point.

The member who brought forth the motion is entitled to speak first. The chair recognizes the member, who stands and presents his case for the motion at hand. After the author of the motion speaks, other members of the assembly wishing to speak may stand, address the chairman, and wait to be recognized by the chairman. Once recognized, they may offer their statements to the assembly.

During the debate, secondary motions, such as those discussed earlier in this chapter, may be offered. The secondary motions must always be resolved before the debate on the original main motion resumes. This is critical because these secondary motions may consist of amendments or alterations to the motion, and of course, making any amendments *before* the motion is carried is much easier and more expedient than waiting to change it later.

Assuming your organization is unlike the U.S. Congress and not starkly divided along partisan lines, there soon comes a point in the discussion at which no one else has anything to say about the motion at hand. The chairperson then "puts the question" to the group by restating the motion "to hire a gardener to remove the weeds from the flowerbed." This is a very important step, restating the motion at hand, because if anyone stepped out of the meeting, or was day dreaming or what have you, then he needs to be sure he's voting on the right motion.

The way votes are tallied, unless there are motions on the floor requesting the use of a specific type of vote, is up to the chairman's discretion. As a best practice, unless there's a clear line of contention surrounding a motion, using the verbal "yay" and "nay" voting helps things run a bit faster in your meetings. Usually those in favor of the motion are called upon first. Afterwards, the "nays" have their chance to sound off.

After the vote is taken the chairman announces the result by saying, "The motion passes/fails," "The motion is carried/is lost" or "The yays/ nays have it." The chairman must then *again* reiterate the substance of the motion: "Organization X will hire a gardener to remove the weeds from the flowerbed." If anyone thinks that the chair is incorrect in her pronouncement of the results, then he may call for a division in which—as discussed previously in this chapter—a standing or written vote is taken.

# | 5 |
# Ways to Create Great Committees

The first chapter of this book established a fictional organization and appointed a committee to draft its bylaws. Preparing bylaws is really just the beginning when it comes to leveraging the value of committees within the organization. Committees are unique in that they're smaller in size versus the body of your organization-at-large. Committee members have been selected according to how well their talents suit a specific task, and the specialization and narrow focus of their purposes means that committees can usually accomplish a great deal in less time than it would take if the task were assigned to the entire organization.

A standard committee, usually established in the bylaws, is charged with a specific, continual function within an organization. Alternatively, a special committee is established for a fixed, temporary term to assess, investigate and report on a particular issue.

> *The ideal committee is one with me as chairman, and the other members in bed with flu.*
>
> – LORD MILVERTON

## Appointing a Committee Chairman

Regardless of the type of the committee, it usually requires a person to act as the committee chairman. Whenever the group acts to establish a certain committee, electing or appointing the chair is the first matter of business. The chairman of a committee can be either appointed by the organization's president or board, or he may be voted in—the particulars should be covered in your bylaws. The chairman should have knowledge in the subject matter on which the committee is focused, as should the rest of the membership.

## Examples of Standing Committees

These are a few examples of the types of committees that can benefit most any organization on a permanent basis.

## Budgetary Committees

Many organizations throw around a lot of cash and benefit from the focused attention of a committee dedicated to preparing budgets, analyzing credit options, and helping the organization keep a healthy cash position. Appointing the organization's treasurer to chair the budgetary committee is a good idea.

## Nominating Committees

In larger organizations especially, the question of who should hold the reigns is very important, as the right leadership can make or break a group. As a result, nominating committees are commonly used to assess candidates for leadership positions. Depending on the nature of these organizations, those nominated for leadership positions need not always come from within the organization's current membership.

## Membership Committee

Organizations don't exist without members. A lagging membership creates all types of problems financial and reputation-related; not to mention that fewer members means there are fewer resources to tap when selecting members and chairs for important committees, like the Membership Committee. It's all a vicious cycle!

In addition to these generic examples of *standing committees*, consider establishing standing committees that specifically benefit your organization. Think about it this way: in what areas does your organization need constant attention? For example, if you're an organization of volunteer firefighters, then you likely want to create a maintenance committee to ensure that all the equipment in the fire station stays in good working order. If you're a Greek fraternity, then you probably want to create a risk management committee to educate the members on alcohol abuse and how to refrain from doing stupid things. If you're a bird watching club, then perhaps a travel committee can regularly be on the lookout for opportunities to join up with bird watching escapes around the world.

# Special Committees

Let's say your organization is in a lot of debt, and after the group votes to depose the treasurer, you need to figure out the most optimal way of paying it back. A special, debt servicing committee could come in handy here. As a special committee, it would only exist for a fixed amount of time, and it would be charged with attending to one specific problem.

Another example: a square dance club's caller passes away. The club needs to find a new caller to bring an audio system and record to the square dance club and call the dances, but they're expensive and they're scarce. A special 'caller recruiting committee' could be formed to attend to the task.

The disbandment of a special committee depends on a few different factors. Robert's Rules provide some ideas on how special committees can be evaporated.

**SUGGESTED REASONS TO DISSOLVE SPECIAL COMMITTEES**

GRAPHIC

fig. 9

- Once the committee clearly completes the task for which it was formed.
- When the assembly that formed the committee formally disbands it. This may happen due to the committee's persistent ineffectiveness or due to changing circumstances rendering the committee's purpose no longer pertinent.
- When the deliberative assembly that formed the committee disbands committee also ceases to exist.

# Establishing Committee Membership

It's important that the members of your committees are suited to the nature of the committee. Robert's Rules provides an assortment of various ways by which committee members may be appointed or voted into existence.

## Appointment Methods

One of the quickest, though most non-participatory, ways to establish a committee's members is to write in the names of the members in the motion which establishes the committee: "It's hereby resolved that a committee should be formed to oversee the community rehabilitation projects sponsored by our society, and that this committee be manned by Robert Jones, Blake Bradshaw, and Lori Steinbern, with Lori Steinbern as the committee chairman." If the motion passes as is, then a committee is established. If a member thinks that the committee is a good idea but would like more deliberation on the membership—perhaps he wants to be included in the committee—then he can make a secondary motion for a division of the question (see the previous chapter).

Committee members may also be appointed through the bylaws of the organization itself. For example, if the organization is very focused on community service, then the community rehabilitation project committee may need to be chaired by the organization's president per the dictates of the bylaws.

The chairman may also appoint committee members in some cases. The right of the chairman to make these appointments can be secured in a variety of ways. Someone can make a motion: "It's resolved that the chairman be responsible for appointing the members and chair of a new special committee devoted to the society's community rehabilitation projects." In another case, the bylaws may specify that the organization has certain standing committees and that the members of these committees (or some of the members) may be appointed directly by the organization's chair.

### Election Methods

If you'd rather have committee members serving under a popular mandate, then they can be formally elected in a few ways. Secret ballot elections are often used when the committee is particularly prestigious and there's fierce competition for a seat. Open nominations, a less formal method, take nominations from the floor. Let's say there are open positions on your organization's finance committee and your friend and fellow member, Tim, is a talented accountant. During open nominations, you would simply shout out: "I nominate Tim."

Once all nominations have been made, the nominees have a chance to speak, making their cases for the position on the committee or the chairmanship, and then everyone votes. The voting can be done by voice, especially if there's apparent unanimous consent. The chairman may also submit a list of nominees to the group for a vote.

## Meeting with Your Committee

According to Robert's Rules, the chairman is responsible for setting up meetings for the committee, but if he fails to do so, then any two committee members may act in his stead and call a meeting. When it comes to giving adequate notice for these meetings and establishing a valid quorum, the same rules apply to committees as apply to the greater organization.

The purpose of the committee is to provide a smaller, more flexible environment in which to operate while holding to a particular focus. The environment of a committee is typically more relaxed. Maintaining and recording notes (or minutes) on your meetings is a good idea, but not always necessary. Usually the committee chair just takes the notes himself. If the committee is exceptionally large, then you may have to default back to the rules of order that your larger organization follows, and rather than have the committee chairman take notes, he may need to assign that task to another individual.

The responsibilities of a committee depend on the mandates set forth for the committee either by the bylaws or by a written motion. But, generally speaking, committees are usually charged with providing a thoughtful report to inform certain key decisions that the greater group faces.

# | 6 |
# A Parliamentary Procedure Sample

Since we've spent so much time talking about the ins and outs of parliamentary procedure, let's put all of that information into practice with an annotated example. So without further ado, let's get into it.

## Order of Business

The **chair** calls the meeting to **order**. If there is any business to be completed for this meeting, a quorum must be present. The size of a quorum for your organization is established in your charter or bylaws.

The **chair** announces that the **secretary** will read the last meeting's **minutes**, and the secretary proceeds to do so. The **chair** puts the question, "Are there any corrections to the minutes?" to the assembly. Normally corrections are suggested without motion or vote. When this process has come to a conclusion, the **chair** announces that the minutes will stand as read or stand as corrected, whichever the case may be.

The **chair** announces and introduces the reports of any **standing committees** or **special committees**. Because the content of these reports often brings new information to light, it is a good idea for the assembly to hear their reports before moving on to the decisions that such information informs.

If a committee report contains a recommendation or other actionable information, the reporting member of that committee, or the **chair**, moves that the recommendation be adopted or that the action be acted upon in some way. If no such action is necessary, the report is filed without action.

The **chair** then addresses **unfinished business** with the question, "Is there any unfinished business?" If there is, action should be made on that business to settle it. The action of postponing a decision through a motion qualifies as settling business. In fact, this can be prudent if a situation is developing but does not require immediate action. The best decision is an informed one, and acting without a full command of all the facts can be detrimental to an organization.

Once unfinished business is settled, the **chair** addresses **new business**. New business is represented by motions that must be discussed and settled before moving forward. This is when members of an assembly can exercise all of those great motions (assuming they have a second). New business can be submitted to the chair and the assembly via motions. An example introduction is outlined below. Note that it is proper nomenclature to describe unfinished business as such. The term "old business" implies that the business in question has already been settled, and is therefore technically incorrect. Unfinished business is business that was never settled or resolved from the last meeting.

## Main Motion

*"Mr./Madame Chair..."*

> *"The chair recognizes Mr. Smith."*

*"I move to introduce the proposal that this organization release an additional $500 in discretionary funds for recruitment efforts."* This motion requires a second; that is to say, someone else who agrees that $500 would be wisely spent on recruitment.

*"I second the motion."* A motion that has a second can now be included in the business of the meeting and can be discussed and voted upon.

> *"The motion has been made by Mr. Smith and seconded by Mrs. Jones. Is there any discussion?"* The chair acknowledges that the motion has a second and can be included in the meeting's discussion.

Here the motion can be changed by amendment in the same way that it was introduced.

*"Mr./Madame Chair..."*

> *"The chair recognizes Mr. Cooper."*

*"I move to amend the motion by changing the release of funds from a value of $500 to only $300 for recruitment of members."*

*"I second the motion to amend."*

> *"It has been proposed that the motion should be amended by reducing the value of funds released from $500 to $300. Is there any discussion?"*

Once the motion has been discussed, the **chair** announces the intention to vote and restate the motion. Restatement of the motion is important as it keeps the meeting on track and ensures that any members that haven't been following along are on the same page as everyone else. Additionally, the statement of the effect that the amendment will have on the motion is important to keep all members and to keep the meeting on track.

*"If there is no further discussion, the motion is a proposal to release funds totaling $500 for member recruitment."* This a final opportunity for amendments; remember that silence is consent when discussing business.

The *chair* puts the motion to a vote using the method outlined in your organization's bylaws or that is appropriate for the motion.

*"All in favor please say 'aye'."* The votes in favor of the motion are tallied.

*"All opposed, please say 'nay'."* The votes against the motion are tallied.

*"The ayes/nays have it. The motion is carried/defeated."*

Once all business is concluded, the meeting returns to the **order of business**. The chair addresses announcements with a simple question: *"Are there any announcements?"*

Once announcements are settled, the **chair** announces the intent to adjourn the meeting.

*"If there is no further business, the meeting will be adjourned."* If no new business is presented, then the meeting is adjourned. If the assembly wishes to adjourn before the meeting's business is completed, this must be done via a seconded motion.

For quick reference, please see the chart on the following page for a summary of order of business procedure.

## The Role of the Chairman

The chair-person plays an integral and pivotal role in the orderly conduct and fair proceeding of meetings. Without an effective chairperson meetings can easily fall off track, and what was a regimented and productive meeting can descend into a bout of gainsaying. It is also key that the meeting's chair remain impartial, as bias on the part of the chair is inimical and counterproductive to the parliamentary process.

GRAPHIC

fig. 10

> *To become an effective Chair, the individual must establish goodwill, respect, and trust between the Chair and the assembly.*
>
> – HUGH CANNON

## Responsibilities of the Chair

1. Calls the meeting to order.

2. Keeps the meeting and the assembly focused on the order of business and the business at hand.

3. Handles the assembly's discussion in an orderly way. This means:
   a. Giving every member time to speak, and ensuring that others don't infringe upon his or her time.

b. Ensuring that speakers adhere to the rules of order, the question at hand, and the current business.

c. Providing impartial and bias-free opportunities for speakers who are both for and against the topic at hand.

**NOTE**

In the instance of large assemblies, a chairperson may employ a gavel to ensure that his or her wishes are known to the assembly. In addition to being very fun, wielding a gavel comes with its own set of rules and common practices. Commonly a single rap of the gavel is used to call the meeting to order, maintain order if the discussion gets out of hand, or declare adjournment.

4. Effective chairs do not enter the discussion and do not interject their own opinions into the assembly's discussion.

a. There are exceptions to this rule, such as when the chairperson's vote would break a deadlock, or whenever a vote is decided by ballot.

5. It is the responsibility of the chair to announce each motion before it is discussed and when it is voted upon. The chair also puts the motions to a vote and announces the outcome.

6. The chair may assist in the wording or formation of motions if the author requests it.

a. For this reason—and many other apparent ones—the chairperson should have a good grasp of parliamentary procedure.

7. The chair may appoint committees when appropriate and if such action is authorized by the bylaws or charter.

It is generally recognized as proper etiquette for the chair to remain seated except during the following circumstances:

» When calling the meeting to order
» When putting a question to a vote
» When deciding on a point of order
» When recognizing speakers

# The Role of the Secretary

Though the secretary doesn't have the same authority and hands-on approach that the chairperson has, the role of the secretary is no less critical to an orderly parliamentary procedure. Decisions made based on inaccurate records are themselves inaccurate, and it behooves an organization to appoint or elect a qualified and expert secretary.

## Responsibilities of the Secretary

1. Keeping an accurate record of each meeting, including the minutes.
    a. These details include the kind of meeting (regular, special, etc.); the name of the assembly; the date, time, and place of the meeting; the name and title of the presiding officer, and if a quorum has been reached.
    b. Approval of previous minutes.
    c. Records of reports and records of main motions along with the member that put them to the assembly, as well as all other motions.
    d. Records of points to order and appeals.
    e. Records of counted votes.
    f. Time of adjournment.

The secretary should sign and date all reports of the meeting. The secretary has the additional responsibilities listed below:

2. Maintaining an up-to-date roll of members.

3. Maintaining up-to-date copies of the charter/constitution and bylaws including any amendments.

4. Maintaining a record of all committees.

5. Providing a list of pending and potential business for the chair before each meeting.

6. Unless there is a designated correspondence secretary, the general secretary handles organizational correspondence. This includes notifying members for meetings, especially for special meetings.

## Some Guidelines Concerning the Record of Minutes

When recording the minutes of a meeting, it is the secretary's responsibility to record what is done, not what is said. These notes should be in a designated place and should be kept together—whether in a special notebook or a marked computer file (that is backed up). It is a best practice to keep the minutes clear and legible. For example, each motion should have its own paragraph so that the minutes can be easily reviewed if necessary.

Minutes should be read and approved during the next meeting, though if meetings are spaced far apart, it can be a good idea to approve and finalize the meeting's minutes before the adjournment of the current meeting rather than let incorrect minutes stand for a long period of time. Letting incorrect minutes stand opens the door for misinterpretation down the road or allows a failure to include pertinent information to go unnoticed.

When presenting a meeting's minutes to the assembly for review, the minutes should be either typed or legibly printed in ink. Corrections or revisions should not hinder their reading or hamper comprehension. All records of minutes should be stored together. Traditionally the longhand, or finalized, minutes are kept in a book form: either loose leaves that are bound or transferred into a records book. It is a best practice to leave wide margins so that corrections or revisions can be entered easily without defacing the content.

# Common Mistakes: Using Parliamentary Language

With many unfamiliar terms and misconceptions surrounding parliamentary procedure as laid down by Robert's Rules, as well as some misinterpretations portrayed in books and movies, it is common for those new to structure to misspeak. The following is a summary of some common mistakes and their corrections to keep you looking your best in front of your colleagues.

*"So moved!"*

While you may have seen this statement used on a TV show, in the real world it has no practical application. Effective and orderly meetings are run with precise language, and the announcement that a motion is "so moved" is vague and ambiguous at best.

Instead, a chairperson should briefly and succinctly state the motion and declare it moved so that there is no confusion from the assembly as to what is being discussed and what has been moved.

*"I move to table."*

The proper phrasing is "move to lay on the table". Additionally, this is not used to permanently kill a motion. That is the movement to postpone indefinitely. Laying a motion on the table is a temporary interruption of the agenda, not a way to quash a motion definitively.

*"Question!"*

"Question" or the "call for question" is often misconstrued as a motion. In truth, a person calling "question" over and over again is being disorderly. Some members of the assembly may use this pseudo 'motion' to push the chair into voting without first hearing debates, discussions, or motions for amendment.

While a genuine motion exists to call the motion to a vote preemptively, shouting "question, question" over and over again is not the right way to go about parliamentary procedure. "I move the main question" as a motion requires a majority vote of two thirds.

## Four Motions that are Always Out of Order

In addition to common mistakes or errors based on ignorance of procedure (or a less savory intent), there are some circumstances in which no matter how firm the will of the assembly, no matter unanimity, these motions will not hold (figure 11).

The first condition is more or less self-explanatory. If something is illegal, then it is illegal, and any action taken outside the law exposes the organization to legal ramifications. The same thing goes for the organization's bylaws: a motion cannot stand if it is in violation of the organization's charter, constitution, or bylaws. If these kinds of motions were allowed, what would be the point of having bylaws?

The second condition exists largely for the sake of brevity. It prevents the creation of 'double work' and keeps the meeting on the path of addressing new and pertinent business. Additionally, if a member of the assembly decided that he was unhappy with the outcome of a vote, he could continuously introduce motions to revisit settled business and effectively hijack the discussion.

Instead, since the business was already settled, the chair can call that member as disorderly and invalidate his motion—assuming it does indeed fit the criteria of having already been rejected. This does not invalidate motions to amend; however, doing so would fly in the face of the entire parliamentary process.

Likewise, the second condition exists to prevent meetings from being derailed. The purpose of a meeting is to determine the will of the assembly; if the assembly is running a hamster wheel discussing the same topic ad nauseam, then the discussion is not productive and could lead to considerable amounts of unfinished business.

The fourth condition is a matter of practicality. While motions may be passed for which there is no existing bylaw of governance, it is imprudent for the organization to make commitments that are far beyond not only organizational capability, but necessity and reasonable accommodation.

GRAPHIC

fig. 11

### LEGAL CONFLICT

- Motions that are in conflict with federal, state, or local laws cannot stand.
- This also applies to the organization's charter and bylaws.

### PREVIOUS REJECTION

- Motions that present something previously rejected during the same session cannot stand.

### SAME QUESTION

- Motions that substantially present the same question are in effect subverting the structure of the meeting and of the organization.

### BEYOND SCOPE

- Motions beyond the scope of the organization's bylaws cannot stand.
- These may be passed regardless, and the bylaws may be amended to fit.

Four motions that will not hold.

# Conclusion

Brigadier General Henry Martyn Robert was a talented engineer, and it's no accident that *Robert's Rules of Order* has survived and retained its prominence for several generations. Robert's Rules provide a very powerful, logic-based skeletal framework for running an organization's deliberative assemblies. When used correctly, Robert's Rules allow the organization to grow and develop, bringing the best ideas to the surface, even if they originate from more quiet personalities. Robert's Rules protect the voices of minorities and ensure that even those who don't actively participate in the group always have an open door.

If you've ever heard of the "80/20" principle, which posits that 20% of the membership in any organization usually does 80% of the work, while 80% does 20% of the work, then you may notice its relevance when incorporating Robert's Rules into your organization. You may find yourself being the one who continually scrambles to get everyone into a meeting so that quorum can be established. You may be chairing multiple committees while others seem to just stand idly by.

Though Robert's Rules isn't a motivational tool—those could fill a book all their own—it allows the busier members of your organization to stay active while keeping opportunities open for members who decide they want to step up and take active roles. Meanwhile, members who like to complain a lot more than they like to work are never able to say that they weren't given ample opportunity to participate in the group's functions. Keep in mind that at any given meeting, any member of that 80% has the right to author and submit a motion, to volunteer to work on a committee, or to otherwise participate actively in the meeting.

If you find that Robert's Rules are really working well for you and would like to expand their application in your group, you can always consider hiring a specialized parliamentarian. Or you can look for educational community programs on Robert's Rules or other forms of parliamentary procedure.

## To continue your education, here are a few resources:

The National Association of Parliamentarians
213 South Main St. Independence, MO 64050-3850
**Phone:** 888-627-2929 | **Website:** www.parliamentarians.org

American Institute of Parliamentarians
550M Ritchie Hwy, #271 Severna Park, MD 21146
Phone: 888-664-0428 | Website: www.parliamentaryprocedure.org

# REMEMBER TO DOWNLOAD YOUR FREE DIGITAL ASSETS!

 Helpful Motions Cheat Sheet

 Sample Minutes Reporting Form

 Golden Triangle Summary

 Sample Meeting Agenda

## TWO WAYS TO ACCESS YOUR FREE DIGITAL ASSETS

**Use the camera app on your mobile phone**
to take a picture of the QR code or visit the link below
and instantly access your digital assets.

**SCAN ME**

or

www.clydebankmedia.com/roberts-assets

**VISIT URL**

# About ClydeBank Media

We create simplified educational tools that allow our customers to successfully learn new skills in order to navigate this constantly changing world.

The success of ClydeBank Media's value-driven approach starts with beginner-friendly high-quality information. We work with subject matter experts who are leaders in their fields. These experts are supported by our team of professional researchers, writers, and educators.

Our team at ClydeBank Media works with these industry leaders to break down their wealth of knowledge, their wisdom, and their years of experience into small and concise building blocks. We piece together these building blocks to create a clearly defined learning path that a beginner can follow for successful mastery.

At ClydeBank Media, we see a new world of possibility. Simplified learning doesn't have to be bound by four walls; instead, it's driven by you.

*Your World. Simplified.*™

# Glossary

**Adjourned Meeting**
A meeting that picks up where a previous meeting left off in terms of processing a certain order of business.

**Annual Meeting**
A deliberative assembly or other meeting that occurs once a year and is often used to conduct specific types of business, such as the nomination and election of new officers, board members, and the hearing of annual reporting on the organization's welfare.

**Board**
A deliberative assembly created for the purpose of management that either reports to a larger deliberative assembly or is autonomous by way of a law or charter.

**Bylaws**
The agreed upon rules an organization uses to govern itself. These rules cannot be changed without a two-thirds vote. In organizations using Robert's Rules of Order, the "bylaws" also encompass any rules set forth by the group in a formal constitution.

**Call or "Call of the Meeting"**
A formal term referring to the issuance of notice for an upcoming meeting. If the call is being given for a special meeting, then the business at-hand must be specified.

**Chairman**
Refers to the person who presides over a group or committee.

**Charter**
Refers to the system of rules established by a parent organization that a subsidiary organization must follow. Also used to refer to formal articles of incorporation as issued by a state authority.

**Debate**
Regulated discourse on a proposed motion.

**Deliberative Assembly**
A group that discusses, debates, and decides on action to be undertaken on behalf of the group at-large.

**Executive Session**
A meeting or group of meetings that's not open to attendees outside the group's membership.

**General Order**
A business item that was postponed in a prior meeting and needs to be heard in the current meeting. This could be an item that was being discussed but was never voted on at the point that the previous meeting adjourned.

## Incidental Motions

Motions that refer to the use and interpretation of the rules of order in a deliberative assembly, such as motions to appeal, motions to suspend the rules, or motions to divide the question.

## Main Motion

The baseline movement of a deliberative assembly: A fundamental call to action on a particular business item.

## Mass Meeting

Refers to an organization of individuals who share a common goal but have yet to agree upon any formal organizational structure for their collective pursuit. Examples would be a town hall assembly, open to all citizens who are concerned about the poor quality of water in the city.

## Motion

A course of action proposed in a meeting.

## Order of Business

A phrase of somewhat loose interpretation meant to convey the increments of business pursued in a parliamentary-style forum or organization. Examples of an order of business include the discussion and voting on a motion, the administering of an election, or the pursuit of a particular business agenda.

## Parliamentarian

A consultant to or permanent officer of an organization whose formal role is to advise the group on matters of parliamentary procedure.

## Parliamentary Law

A general set of common-sense rules that govern the conduct of deliberative assemblies.

## Privileged Motion

A type of secondary motion that doesn't relate directly to the substance of the main motion currently on the floor, but instead focused on the logistics of running the meeting.

## Quorums

A requisite minimum number of members who must be present in order for an organization's meeting to be considered legally valid.

## Ratify

When the group approves after the fact, following an action taken by a group member without proper authorization.

## Regular Meeting

A meeting of a group, designated by the group's bylaws or a standing rule, that occurs on a regular basis—daily, weekly, bi-weekly, etc.

## Resignation

Refers to stepping down from one's official duties as an organization's officer, board member, executive director or committee chairman. Usually requires adequate notice given and fulfillment of all regular obligations until the group formally accepts the resignation. Resignations can be sought after in the form of a proposed motion.

## Resolution for Permanent Association

A written document that demonstrates an assembly's intent to become a solidified organization. Prior to having such a resolution, the assembly is not bound by bylaws or parliamentary procedure.

## Secondary Motion

A motion that supports the group's processing of a main motion, including subsidiary motions, privileged motions, and incidental motions.

## Seconding

A verbal affirmation in support of a new motion. Some motions require seconds in order to be heard and considered by the assembly, and others do not.

## Session

One or a series of meetings intended to pursue a specific order of business.

## Special Committee

A committee that's established for a fixed, temporary term to assess, investigate and report on a particular issue.

## Special Meeting

A meeting summoned outside of the regular meeting schedule, usually to address a specific concern facing the group. Special committees are sometimes referred to as "select" or "ad hoc" committees.

## Special Order

An item of business that, due to a motion, or because it's written into the bylaws, is scheduled to be heard at a specific meeting. Special orders usually take precedence over all other business at a regular meeting.

## Special Rule of Order

Special rules of order are exceptions and exemptions that are written into an organization's bylaws to determine when and how the organization differs from its procedural guide of choice—such as Robert's Rules. Special rules of order, when officially adopted as part of the bylaws, are just as valid for that organization as any other bylaws or parts of the organization's charter.

## Standing Committees

A committee, usually established in the bylaws, charged with a specific, continual function within an organization.

**Standing Rules**

Rules not specified in the bylaws, constitution, charter, or rules of order, that govern an organization's process. Standing rules are voted in by a majority and may be suspended at a later time, but only during the normal course of a meeting during which their application arises.

**Subsidiary Motion**

A motion put forth to alter or help expedite the processing of a main motion, such as a motion to amend or a motion to send to committee.

# Notes

Made in United States
Orlando, FL
31 March 2023